THE KNIFE
and
other poems

THE WESLEYAN POETRY PROGRAM : VOLUME 100

THE KNIFE
and
other poems.

RICHARD TILLINGHAST

Wesleyan University Press
Middletown, Connecticut

7/1981
Am. Lit. Cont.

Acknowledgment is gratefully made to the following periodicals,
in the pages of which these poems originally appeared:
Floating Island, "Legends about Air & Water"
The Gayoso Street Review, "Borders, Woven Goods, and the Rhythm behind
All Things," "Lost Cove & The Rose of San Antone," "Summer Rain"
Missouri Review, "Aspens and a Photograph," "Return"
New Letters, "Shooting Ducks in South Louisiana"
The New Republic, "Control," "Hearing of the End of the War," "The Knife"
Paris Review, "Sovereigns"
Partisan Review, "Blue"
Ploughshares, "Eight Lines by Jalal-ud-din Rumi," "Things Past"
Sumac, "My Ghost," "The Thief "

In England: *Agenda*, "Legends about Air & Water"
Critical Quarterly, "The Knife," "Return," "Shooting Ducks in South Louisiana"
An earlier version of "Shooting Ducks in South Louisiana" appeared in
Ten American Poets, ed. James Atlas, Carcanet Press, Cheshire, England.

"Just Like Tom Thumb's Blues," Music and Lyrics by Bob Dylan,
Copyright © 1965, Warner Bros., Inc. All Rights Reserved. Used by permission.

Library of Congress Cataloging in Publication Data

Tillinghast, Richard.
  The knife, and other poems.

  (Wesleyan poetry program ; v. 100)
  I. Title.
PS3570.I38K54   811'.54   80-18826
ISBN 0-8195-2100-0
ISBN 0-8195-1100-5 (pbk.)

Distributed by Columbia University Press
136 South Broadway, Irvington, NY 10533

Manufactured in the United States of America
First edition

To
MARTHA WILLIFORD TILLINGHAST
and
RAYMOND CHARLES TILLINGHAST
My mother and father

Contents

I

Return : 11
The Thief : 15
My Ghost : 17
Control : 18
Eight Lines by Jalal-ud-din Rumi : 19
Legends about Air & Water : 21
The Knife : 23
Hearing of the End of the War : 26
Aspens and a Photograph : 29
Shooting Ducks in South Louisiana : 30
Lost Cove & The Rose of San Antone : 32
Blue : 34
Things Past : 36
Borders, Woven Goods, and
   the Rhythm behind All Things : 38
Summer Rain : 42

II

Sovereigns : 47
Views of the Indies : 48
Today in the Café Trieste : 52

I

Return

1.

Sunburst cabbage in grey light
                summer squash bright as lemons
red tomatoes splitting their skins
          five kinds of chilis burning in cool darkness,
        sunflower lion's-heads
                  in the blue Chevy pickup.

Hands shaking from the cold
              turn on the headlights; he starts
                    down the drive—

A dust you can't see
          settles over the garden and empty cabin

              silent, unnoticed
           like snow after midnight—

Power shut off in the pumphouse
           tools suspended over light-blue silhouettes
         he has painted for each of them.

Dark trees stand
         and watch his old truck
                bump down the hill.

Behind him: star-fall he's not sure he saw,
       bone-chill flute
             certainty of dawn.

He feels the pecans, the wild hazelnuts
                  the small but hard and juicy apples
            in the oversized pockets of his coat,
                  the cloth worn soft as rabbit-fur.

White dairy-fences border his way,
                  AM radio farm news,
            placidness of black-nosed sheep in ground-fog,
                  mist rising over bluegrass.

He drives by Tomales Bay.
            The old fisherman scowls at the low sky and waves,
                  squinting to keep out the
                  wreathing, first-cigarette smoke.

      Squirrels
            flash down tree-trunks
when they see him coming—
                  Farmers turn on their lights.

Seeds sprout in the upholstery.
                        Tendrils and runners leap out
            from under his dashboard—

He sails past the whitewashed stumps
                        from the 1906 earthquake,
past the old hotel at Olema,
                  stops for a whizz at Tocaloma,
            because of the name.

Sycamore leaves are falling,
            I feel them rustling
around his shoulders
            and wreathing his hair.

The shepherd with eyes like his
            wakes up in a field.
    The farmer goes out to milk,
        his cold hands pink on the pink freckled udders.

The fisherman he could almost be
            lets down nets into dark water

        and brings up the trout-colored dawn.

2.

For a few miles on the freeway we
                    float in the same skin,
        he and I.
                    But the sun rises in my
    rearview mirror.
        I'm myself now.
I cross the bridge and pay my toll.

The city draws me like a magnet—
            first the oil refineries,
the mudflats and racetrack by the Bay,
                the one-story houses,
then a vision of you waking up:
            cheeks reddening, your black hair long,
your eyes that remind me of Russia,
                        where I've never been—
        as you look out at
                silvery rain on the fuchsias.

I find your house by feel.
        How many years are gone?
Your name is gone from the mailbox.
The tropical birds and palm trees and Hawaiian sunset
            you painted with a small brush
are peeling off the beveled glass door.

Forever must be over.
I get into the truck with the good things
            somebody has left here,
                    and drive off into the rain—
my left hand asking my right
                a question I could never answer.

14

The Thief

The thief came down
    through the avenue of dreams.
He took my battered gold,
    my blood-hued jewels from before
        the Revolution—
things I could never get back—

And the vine-covered jungle temple
    that the blind lady told me about:
my sword in one hand,
    in one hand the steaming, bloody virgin heart
        still beating . . .

In the days after,
    on the dusty backroads and crossroads
        in the palms of my hands,
the salt-sweat stars glistened
        at midday;
I felt the speckled wisdom
of East Anglian saints and elders,
    the Word in the shadow of a doorway,
the world swaying in a pail of well-water.

The bees sang in the pines,
    loud in the sunlit open places.

I wake in a cold halo of sweat.
But wasn't I awake already?—
trembling and glancing around in fright
    like deer in the canyon
which also are gone,
crashing off gazelle-like into the trees.

Glass shattered out all around me,
     glass stuck to my fingers,
I'm wiping my eyes—

It's really gone!
I'm sitting up in bed.

Through the huge smashed pane,
     moon over ocean pasture,
Pacific roaring over me.

I'm grinning and bowing like Old Fezziwig
and shaking the hands of flies and bees
     as they pick through the remnants.

Many things that were mine
          are gone.
In my sleep the cat comes purring.
His happiness is, he says,
          as important as mine.
And in sleep comes the thief

leaving me in the care of
the little blind lady in the sunset
and the Chinese postmaster
and the man who says
     "Stay afterward.
I have an introduction for you
that will make everything clear."

My Ghost

AFTER BAUDELAIRE

The archangel of flaming air
  a beast's eyes in my exploded head
I'm coming back to you
        forcing the stairs to exist
pretending my feet can touch the ground

  Coming to you
on the black side of the moon
     where you lie
        in the far oasis of your mind

Coming to you like a crystal ship through polar swamps
      like a long-nosed jungle snake
         gliding
      into your hot grave.

When morning comes,
      bruised and blood-drained,
       you turn to me in bed and
    the space I occupy is empty.

What your other men want
       leaves me cold.
I want you out of your mind with wanting,
    terrified   beautifully
      of the blood that presses against your heart   Then

       I ride flesh again
    and the blown cells flash with life.

Control

Spider fleeing
    from web-eye to twig
in fear of my breath

Deer cringing in bracken
    Hare's long ear-veins
        thud.
    at your foot-crash

Clam's mouth full of oil.

    Even the unchangeable
Redwood
    tenses its billowy fronds
when the Human stops too near.

Axe-concussion
    chainsaw nerve-bite
the cruelty of children

    while the moon
        feeds
on man after man.

Eight Lines by Jalal-ud-din Rumi

Leaving here, I slip out the gates of the palace garden
    as autumn stuns the trees with remembrance
        and makes them come around again

          —a memory of dervish flutes—

In my mind I hear the word *perfect*.
        My feet touch down into cool dust
          and my eyes look up
to the mountains that ring the high plateau—

Perfect the way air is,
    including everything there is
        that one can pass through:

The shadow-wings of seabirds
glide over storm-clouds   forming and dissolving
          turning to the unseen.

And no one really knows
    what keeps one from going too:

        sleeping under leaves
dissatisfied and hungry   praying to the Great Light
      by day, and to the Moon, Our Lady—

      My only friends were the wolves.

A shadow fell from the oldfashioned porchlight,
    called my name into the trees,
and promised to buy me everything.

I was held by the thought of return
and went back far enough to hear the music,
that was once so much a part—
but the cold wind
blew it out of my heart.

I crept unseen one rainy night
into their carriage,
and caressed them in the form of warmth
while they talked happily and drove.

Yet the wind today
spreads yellow leaves across the road
so familiar in the way it disappears
over hills the color of sky—

And the whirlwind dervish voices blow
over desolate stone:

Come, come again, whoever you are
—wanderer, worshiper, lover of leaving—
it doesn't matter.
Ours is not a caravan of despair.
Come even though you have broken your vows
back there
a thousand times—
Come once more.

Legends about Air & Water

When they came down from their mountains:
    spurred feet ungripping rock,
wings becoming useless and a memory,
      then half-a-memory
    of something formal and long ago . . .

Then armor and dust on palace stairs.

      High over green lands
beyond the earth's curve and sense of time
      cliff-dizzy and crest-risen:
    air-masters with a mile to soar—
their wing-strength above any
      word in tongue.

    To live like them!
      To glide on air,
hang weightless in the change of winds—
      ride the pocket of the wave or stream . . .

Slate-stream grey
      of *her* eyes:
    cold water from below the well,
      water that gathers in perfect drops
        at the open mouths of the grass—

Hills made thin
    by the long time I've been dreaming,
worn clear as a membrane-lip of shell.
    Faint blood-beats of music
      from a time lived beyond memory
in the dark ocean fed by her heart.

Day dawns
—red like the first time—
and the ranges of mountains rise,
their curtains of snow pale rose and changing
in the first light.

She leads you like yourself as a child
where the mountain torrent
tosses her hair
like bright water   rainbowed and swift as wings
over rippling gold in the sand.

And tonight you *know*
you would rather be
the little blue bowl at her feet

—as she looks down the valley from her cabin door—

than, over her head,
the starry sky.

The Knife

FOR DAVID TILLINGHAST

What was it I wonder?
   in my favorite weather   in the driving rain
     that drew me like a living hand
What was it
  like a living hand
that spun me off the freeway
     and stopped me
  on a sidestreet in California
with the rain pelting slick leaves down my windshield

to see the words of my brother's poem
     afloat on the bright air,
  and the knife I almost lost
     falling end over end through twenty years
       to the depths of Spring River—

the knife I had used to cut a fish open,
       caught in time
  the instant where it falls
     through a green flame of living water.

My one brother,
     who saw more in the river than water
  who understood what the fathers knew,
       dove from the Old Town canoe
  plunged and found his place
       in the unstoppable live water

seeing with opened eyes
        the green glow on the rocks
                and the willows running underwater—
        like leaves over clear glass in the rain—

While the long-jawed, predatory fish
    the alligator gar
watched out of prehistory
        schooled in the water like shadows
            unmoved in the current,
        watched unwondering.

        The cold raw-boned, white-skinned boy
    curls off his dive in deep water
        and sees on the slab-rock
filling more space than the space it fills:

            the lost thing   *the knife*
        current swift all around it

and fishblood denser than our blood
    still stuck to the pike-jaw knifeblade
which carries a shape like the strife of brothers
                —old as blood—
        the staghorn handle smooth as time.

        Now I call to him
            and now I see
    David burst into the upper air
gasping as he brings to the surface our grandfather's knife
        shaped now, for as long as these words last,
            like all things saved from time.

I see in its steel
  the worn gold on my father's hand
    the light in those trees
the look on my son's face   a moment old

  like the river   old like rain
  older than anything that dies can be.

Hearing of the End of the War

1.

Clouds dissolve into blueness.
    The Rockies float like clouds,
white ridge over blue,
    in the shimmery blue heat.

The moon floats there still
    like some round marble relic,
its classic face rubbed away by time.

A stranger arrives, all the way from Denver.
        We feed him.
He tells us that the war is over.

For years I have stopped to wonder
    what it would feel like now.
And now I only hear the slight noise
       the moment makes,
    like ice cracking,
as it flows behind me into the past.

2.

I go to the well
    and draw up a bottle of homemade beer.
The coldness from thirty feet down
       beads out wet on the brown bottle.

Breathing dusty pine fragrance,
       I pop open the beer, and drink
till my skull aches from the coldness.

Rubbed white dust is on plum skins
                    as they ripen,
                              green wild blueberries
            growing from the rocks.

Wind blows in off the peaks,
                    high in the dust-flecked sun-shafts
            that light up the dark trees.
Rustlings and murmured syllables from other days
                    pass through and linger
                    and leave their ponies
        to roam among the trees and graze the coarse grass
                    off the forest floor.

Treetop breezes, and voices
                    returning home
        from a fight somebody lost in these mountains
                    a hundred and ten years ago—

    A horse cries out,
                    loose in the woods,
                              running and free.
His unshod hooves thud
                    on the hard-packed dirt.

And then each sound drops away
        —like a dream you can't even remember—

    deep behind the leaves of the forest.

3.

From bark-covered rafters
   white sheets hang squarely down,
dividing the still afternoon into rooms
    where we sleep, or read,
     or play a slow game of hearts.

Everyone is unbuttoned and at their ease.

   The baby's clear syllables
      rise into space:
  milky   like the half-moons
    on his tiny fingernails,

       finer than fine paper.

A new life breathes in the world—
     fragile, radiant,
   unused to the ways of men.

From halfway down the valley
    bamboo flute notes rise   float
       flutter
        and shatter
     against the Great Divide.

Aspens and a Photograph

Winding down from fourteen thousand feet
through melting slush and Rocky Mountain tundra,

suddenly: white flesh of new aspens—
              and a photograph I still see
        from an attic in Trinidad,
           Colorado.

Around bends in the road,
             between the blue distances of sky,
         coveys of aspen.
Their leaves flutter all at once in the wind:
         small wing-beats in fear.

Green aspens—tall, root-tough,
  wind-graced and swayed in the blustery weather.
Right up against granite,
    saplings springing up through snow.

The photograph:
two girls' faces from 1881
in a house that raised six generations on silver—
their black gowns, aprons, their Chinese embroidery—
    only daughters
           smiling thinly into the black camera,
holding in their laps, as a kind of joke,
    long-barreled pistols.

Shooting Ducks in South Louisiana

FOR DAVID TILLINGHAST

The cold moon led us coldly
  —three men in a motorboat—
down foggy canals before dawn
    past cut sugarcane in December.

    Mud-banks came alive by flashlight.
Black cottonmouth moccasins
  —the length of a man in the bayou—
slid into black water, head high,
  cocky as you might feel
stepping out on Canal Street
    going for coffee at 4 A.M.
        at the *Café du Monde*.

An Indian trapper called to us
  from his motorized pirogue,
        Cajun French on his radio,—
taking muskrat, swamp rat, weasel,
  "anything with fur."

Marsh life waking in the dark:
gurgling, sneaking, murdering, whooping—
  a muskrat breast-stroking through weeds toward food,
    his sleek coat parted smooth by black satin water—
frogs bellowing, bulbous waterlilies adrift
    cypresses digging their roots into water-borne ooze
dark juices collapsing cell-walls,
        oil rigs flaring thinly at daybreak.

Light dawned in our hunting-nerves.
We called to the ducks in their language.
They circled, set wing, glided into range.
   Our eyes saw keener.
Our blood leaped. We stood up and fired—
   and we didn't miss many that day,
      piling the boat between us with mallards.

The whole town of Cutoff ate ducks that Sunday.
   I sat in the boat,
         bloody swamp-juice sloshing my boots,
            ears dulled by the sound of my gun,—
and looked at a drake I had killed:
   sleek neck hanging limp,
                  green head bloodied,
         raucous energy stopped.
I plucked a purple feather from his dead wing,
and wore the life of that bird in my hat.

Lost Cove & The Rose of San Antone

Evening comes on. I put on a clean white shirt
and feel how well it fits me. I pour bourbon,
with spring water from a plastic jug,
and look out sliding glass doors
at green suburban hills blurred with smog.
Two watches lie on the table before me:
one set for now, one telling time in 1938,
their glass faces reflecting the round California sky.

The man I see through the eye of the second watch
sits in a silence too deep for my nerves
and stares out at twilight
fading on trunks of pine and oak.
The black Model-A car rusts into the stream
that runs past his cabin in Lost Cove, Tennessee.
He reaches for the whiskey on the table,
and his sleeve clears a path through pine-needles and dust.

The coal that tumbles out of his hillside
soils the air and brick houses in Nashville.
Words burn in the rain there
from the power of water that runs past his door.
He looks at his watch and turns on the radio.
The music reaches him, all the way from Nashville.
He holds his glass of whiskey up to the light
that is almost gone. Its color suits his thoughts.

The fiddles and autoharp fill up the dark room
and push out through paint-blackened screens
into black oaks that press against the house.
His face hurts me. It doesn't look right.

He goes against the grain
of whiskey he has made himself, and rides
the wire-song of a steel guitar through small towns,
through the bug-crowded air of farm-crossings late at night.

The disembodied, high guitar line swims in his nerves
like a salmon up a flint-rock stream,
falls like a hawk on blood.
The whiskey burns and soothes.
His tongue starts to move to the words of the song:
trains and big woods and bottomless rivers,
hard drinking, broken hearts, and death.
His blood knows whose song this is.

He's never swum in no bottomless river,
or rode that night train to Memphis,
or sat and stared at those thirteen unlucky bars.
But he sees the moon rise, with the Rose of San Antone
tattooed on it in blood.
A waitress in Denver glides toward him with drinks on a tray.
He stumbles, drunk, through strange woods by an airport
and walks out in San Francisco with a gun in his pocket. . . .

The moon sets, over hills cold and unfamiliar.
I shut off the radio, and hear the sea-roar of the freeway.
Who is this man I have dreamed up?
I cork the bottle, and get up and lock the door.

Blue

AFTER MALLARMÉ

The serene irony of infinite blue—
 beautiful without trying, like blue morning glories,—
unnerves the local poet,
 who pisses away his gift, and just survives
crossing a desert peopled by tragedies.

Running away, my eyes closed, still I feel it gaze,
 with its stone-age remorse, into my transparent soul.
Where is there to run?
 What haggard night can I seize with my hands
to throw, bleeding, in the face of this contempt?

I call the fogs in:
 Release your monotonous powders into the blue,
your ragged lines of snow,
                                    to drown the dark November days.
Put up a white ceiling of silence.

And you! Drift in from oblivious swamps
 just this side of hell—
clutching to you as you come, slime and pale roses—
 You, Precious Boredom, fill with a tireless hand
those great blue holes the birds keep making in the sky.

Let the sad chimneys incessantly smoke!
                         Let a wandering prison of smog
—fear seeping through its black bars—
                    asphyxiate the sun,
morbidly yellow on the horizon.

The sky is dead. Matter, I'm returning to you.
　　　Let this old martyr forget his numberless sins
and even his cruel Ideal,
　　　as he comes to share the straw bed
where the happy human cattle lie.

There, at last, since my brain is used up,
　like an old jar of rouge thrown out with the trash,
and lacks the art to cosmetize
　thoughts that come sobbing to the surface,
there I'll try to yawn myself to death.

No! Blue wins—I hear it sing in the bells.
　My soul, it gives itself a voice
to frighten us even more
　while it pushes us into the ground.
In living steel it sings blue angel-song.

It rolls through the mist, an ancient thing,
　and cuts through your native agony
like a confident sword.
　Where is there to go in this blue and crazy rebellion?
It haunts me! Blue! Blue! Blue! Blue!

Things Past

Ten years into memory, a house
  in the bright fluid
time—dark grain of walnut, dark
women's bodies
    in paintings by sisters.

1632 Walnut Street:
  the solid multiples of eight
    like a vintage Oldsmobile,
the curves of the numbers,
  the porch, the porch-roof lighted,
shaped a little by memory—
  lit up like a jukebox,
like an oldfashioned sunset.

Wood-doves murmur in the eaves
    as we wake.
Leaf-shadows   sun-circles
  glide over the white ceiling
    from outside our lives.
Xoe's German shepherd, "Hussah,"
  lolls sheeplike
among the garden weeds.

On the white terrace
  Ruthie brushes out her thick hair
    straight and blonde.
Between storms: January sunlight
  rare cloud-rainbows
    the air like a telescope
trained on the rain-wet Berkeley hills.

Mexican smoke curls
over the drifting walnut grain.
Sisters, Maurya and Tamara,—
　　your voices, your names!

I drive by the house in the rain
　　　tonight
and see myself at the kitchen table.
As I write,
　　my notebook rests on an open cookbook.
My beard curls
　　in the steamy air
of Christmas turkey soup they are cooking.

Janis Joplin still sings　　*Love*
　　　　　is like a ball and chain!
The guitar solo
　　　　cuts through the years
like a pulsating river of acid.

They're drinking coffee together,
　　and talking about the weather
　　that squally, blowsy Berkeley night.
I can hardly see myself
　　for the steam gathering on the glass.

Borders, Woven Goods, and
the Rhythm behind All Things

The barbs on the barbed-wire fence
that bordered my land in misty rain
burned evilly
downhill through second-growth redwoods.
Deer season: rifle fire in the woods.
The border wind was thick, and colder than reality,
smelling of murder, of the Percys and Douglases
and the troubles in the North.

Maureen made me take off the cap
she had knitted me.
"It's too bright," she said.

The world came apart for the second time.
Benjy stampeded the cattle toward us
with border-dog instincts
curled tight in his fur
like the smoke of fugitive campfires
clinging in highland wool.
Benjy's gold coat shimmered
like a gold Kathmandu temple-dog as he ran.
I saw the cattle charge, double—
their spirits next to them
like their shadows—
bright outlines of blizzard.
We sheltered in that circular
scrub-redwood grove
halfway up the ridge
in the huge, upland, rock-filled pasture,
watching from trees
as they ghosted past with thunder.

"Woven goods are the secret,"
I told you and Maureen gravely.
We were "like family."
"We can't help you,"
you both said sensibly,
and let me lose my mind alone.

Real estate dreams
were the life-force of America,
from Washington on—
the California landscape told me
as I drove up Thursday after work.
The brakes on my little foreign car
slipped on Thursday's cheap, flimsy hills
and steep grades up and down
the road to Point Reyes;
and Paul, I can hear you saying *Point Rey-yez*
as if it were Mexico.
On the radio Bob Dylan was moaning:
"*When* you're lost in the rain in Juarez
and it's Eastertime too!
And your gravity fails
and negativity won't get you through!"

Feather-foot, wing-guided
to her little house down the road,
emerging wide-open from the creek,
the Sonoma remnant of the once-vast forest of redwoods
from San Francisco north to Canada—
to be welcomed as a ghost always expects to be,
with salads from the garden,
love, no questions, old wine.

No, I went on that trip alone.
I rolled in the mud and cow-dung.
I threw away *The Purpose of Life*,
by Hazrat Inayat Khan,
and never found it again.
I lay there in the mire all afternoon
wondering who I was,
watching weekend traffic below on the highway.

My eyesight got perfect
my glasses lost or broken.
I could see everything, 360°,
but I couldn't see who it was
who was seeing it.
Borders, knit, woven things,
the Sunday drivers down below me.

The rhythm of motors.
I clicked my teeth together
and found a rhythm,
one, then two, then two and two,—
and that brought me back into the world.

Woven things. They are warmer than skins.
I like to think of the person who unraveled that,
twisting together sheep's wool and thistles
on some hillside in the early pastoral age.

I walk out in thought with you tonight, Paul,
in the hills where I know you wander,
in the chaparral over Santa Barbara,—
and with you, Maureen,
working at your flower stand, paying for your house . . .
You see me for a moment in the eyes of a customer.
I see Benjy's proud jaws
on buses in Mexico, "the protector,"
when you were pregnant with Amin,—
his silk, curly coat
and his border ancestry.

This is what I wanted to say:
The family is what there is.
Woven things are warmer than skins.
All life is rhythm.
At borders, think.

I think the cows ate that knitted cap.

Summer Rain

Summer rain, and the voices of children
        from another room.
Old friends from summers past,
we drink old whiskey and talk about ghosts.
The rain ebbs, rattles the summer cottage roof,
   soaks the perished leaves in wooden gutters,
then gusts and
        drowns our fond talk.
It's really coming down, we chatter,
   as though rain sometimes rose.
The power fails.
We sit under darkness, under the heavy storm.
Our children—frightened, laughing—
   run in to be beside us.

The weak lights surge on.
We see each other's children newly.
How they've grown!   we prose
with conventional smiles, acceptingly commonplace,
   as they go back to playing.
Yet growing is what a child does.

And ourselves?
You haven't changed a bit,
   we not exactly lie,
meaning the shock is not so great
     as we'd expected.
It's the tired look around the eyes,
the flesh a little loose on the jaw . . .

Your oldest daughter's a senior at Yale.
We're like our grandparents and our parents now,
     shocked by the present:

A buggy without a horse to pull it?
                              A man on the moon?
                Girls at Yale?
We say goodnight. I can hardly lift
    my young son anymore
as I carry him to the car asleep.

The rain comes down, comes down, comes down.
One would think it would wear the earth away.
You told us about a skeleton
    you awoke seeing—
the dawn light on the bone.
It wakes me this morning early.
But I'm sure it wasn't a ghost, you said
        in your sensible way,
It was just my terrible fear of death.

Rain roars on the broad oak leaves
    and wears away the limestone.
I smell the mildewed bindings
    of books I bought as a student.
How shabby, how pathetic they look now
    as they stand there on their shelves unread!
Children are all that matters, you said
    last night, and I agreed.
The children's play-song—repetitive, inane—
    keeps sounding in my head.
I get up—last night's spirits alive
    this morning in my blood—
and write these perishing words down
in the voice of summer rain.

II

Sovereigns

AFTER RILKE

The sovereigns of the world are old,
and die without heirs.
Their pale sons die behind guarded doors.
Their daughters yield weak crowns to violence;
they break in the rough hands of the people.
The haughty, beefcattle faces bleed
   into eagles and hammers.

New money, new metal, new rulers—
the old glitter just beyond reach:
rows of decorations on white dress uniforms.
They reincarnate as gears
to turn the machine of the world.

But luck is beyond possessing.

The metal is wild, and homesick.
Each day is one day less
until it disappears
from the mints and factories
that show it so poor a life.
From bank-vaults, from inside clocks,
in dreams it runs again
through slow arteries inside mountains.
The heart pauses,
and pumps it back to the source.

Views of the Indies

In the kingdom of Jah
Man shall reign.

1.

Azure tropical sky
reflections   in an ocean as green
    as a swimming pool.

Clouds of mist in green camphor trees,
    tin roofs sloping up to mountains.
Miles of refuse and a city:

A cow munching newspapers
      wobbles in traffic—
a hollow carcass blown up with air,
    brushing with her ribs
Chevrolets and Plymouths from the 50s,
   red noise   radio speakers on poles
mangoes stacked in ripe dust.

Pigs root up filth
    out of cracks in the pavement;
a little girl shepherds them.

Blessed are the poor,
    somebody says,
for they live on fire and air—
     weed-cigarettes   cheap rum
         crime   TV
    and the white moon,
    its edges sharp as broken glass.

A squadron of B-52s
    plays a Bach cantata
in a church made entirely of bones.

Blessed are the weak,
for they have to get strong in a hurry.

2.

    Dust-skinned men
    peacock feathers   matted hair
spirit-legs chalk-brown
    gums betel-nut red
   bad-looking eyes.
    They carry a litter.
They hurry   over hard-packed dirt
past tough-rooted old ghosts of trees
    down winding streets.
   The body they carry,—
    insubstantial,
   bundle of orange cloth
    roped to saplings.
The wind turns around:
   hair burning   burning flesh.

Vultures float
    on the heavy air.

Fires to dispose of the dead.

Boats full to the river with firewood.
   Long barges glide past
  with quarried marble and tin ore,
the far bank of the river vague in brown haze.

Riverbank temples:
      harsh, glittering cymbals
            yellow hundreds of candles.

Attendants circle the blazes,
   men the missionaries never met—
long poles in their hands to crack bones
      faces chapped by fire
  eyes shiny, black, unfocused—
They stoke up their *ganja*-pipes with live coals
      off the funeral pyres.

    Gongs beat the thick air.
Black god enthroned on a dead steer.
Black skulls explode in bloodshot eyes.

Souls die in those fires—
    or do the greasy smoke and incense
   the funeral coins clutched in dead hands,
     weird chants of holy widows,
carry them clear over the wide, bending river?

           3.

Like Monarch butterflies the souls glide
      through a garden
where the animals worship them
   and call them the first woman and man.
Now the voice of God.
Now sweat pours down to water the cane.

High lightning zig-zags across the darkness.
The storm breaks.   Monkeys scream
    and crash off into the bush.

The jungle parts around brown, smooth faces:
        Indians
            seeing for the first time
                the City—
        their liquid eyes suddenly still.

Rain beats down the brown smoke
        of cooking fires on mud,
    darkens the stone colonial prison
            heavy in the mist—
        skyscraper walls of corporate glass,
white crosses of missionary churches
        over rain-slick banana leaves,—
            like a tragic warning
        from the incomprehensible past.

Power surges on and off
        through low-voltage bulbs in palm trees,
            throwing dark rainbows into steamy night.
The Indians look into each other's eyes
            and laugh their strange laugh,
                and push each other in play.
They ask, in their birdlike tongue,
        the way to the marketplace.

Today in the Café Trieste

Behind the red lacquered gates,
wine is left to sour, meat to rot.
Outside these gates
lie the bones of the frozen and starved.
The flourishing and the withered
*   are just a foot apart.*
The thought of it is an open wound.

*   —Tu Fu, 8th century*

The Mountain Goddess, if she is still there,
*   will see the world all changed.*

*   —Mao Tse-tung, 1956*

Today in the Café Trieste,
        in San Francisco,
I watch through high rippled windows
        flawed and old
the blue sky that reveals
        and resembles nothing.

A face in the mirror:
    someone else's for an instant
        as I order coffee.
A smile-line cuts the flesh on the left side
        like a scar
    in an otherwise balanced face,
as though everything I've smiled at in thirty-eight years,
        or accepted with irony,
pulled me toward one side of the universe.
My face returns my stare blankly.

I slip back into it.
The light slips off my lenses,
    the marine light of the hot afternoon,
      a little too bright for the wine
  I drank last night.

Mrs. Giotta says something in Italian:
La vita, life—
    or the world, *il mondo,*
      I think she is saying—
  is a solid, well-made glass.
This Italian lady sets a warm glass
        of something
      in front of you,
and you know the world is in order.
When order goes,
glass is the first thing to break.

Mindlessly I watch
    the North Italian daughter-in-law
      open the dishwashing machine
and roll out a tray
    on one-inch plastic wheels—
a tray of dishes like a story
      about the future of the world,
like Buenos Aires' walled-off gardens
      seen from a private plane.
In the upturned tops of green stemware—
    jade lakes, limpid
      half-moons
  of hot water, cooling,
redolent of jungle spring,
    clean steam rising in the café.

The daughter-in-law
    pumps the espresso machine
like a lady engineer
    in the cab of a steam locomotive
in Italy, after the Revolution.

I sit at my favorite table.

September 9, 1976,
    three years ago,
someone else's paper told me
Mao Tse-tung had died,
    ten minutes into that day.
I sat at this same corner table,
    looking at newsprint photos,
        and watched the sky stream away—
    a wooden flagpole,
a Gothic rooftop wobbly in the old glass.

Five Photographs of Mao Tse-tung:

1. *With Chu Teh in Yenan, 1937*

Mao scowls, a cigarette between his light fingers,
as if he has just inhaled
    and is holding his breath—
no rank on his uniform,
    his feet in cloth slippers.
Chu Teh, his best general, straddles the pavement,
    a broken brick by his sneaker.
Happiness spreads from his peasant eyes.
Mao Tse-tung,
        squinting, high-cheeked, cautious,
seems to be analyzing a problem.

2. *Mao Tse-tung with bodyguards,*
during flight from Yenan, 1948

A character from Chinese opera
   —his wife Chiang Ch'ing, "Green River,"
     behind him on a shaggy pony—
inconvenienced, merely
       disdainful of enemy bombers,
   their caravan small in the vast landscape.

Tribesmen in the line of march,
   dark Mongolian bodyguards—
tightness of fear in their faces.

3. *Mao Tse-tung in triumph in Peking,*
October, 1949

Standing up
in a new jeep with good tires,
wearing a black, fur-collared, new-looking coat—
     his face turned toward interminable rows
       of motorized artillery,
     freshly painted barrels raised in salute—
Mao's eyes unfocused into the distance.

4. *Peking, undated*

A human face covering the side of a building,
Mao Tse-tung, not so big as the ear
   of his portrait,
silk-suited, surrounded by diplomats and generals,
  stiffly at attention on a balcony
     over the head of his massive image.

55

Two million people
  in the Place of Heavenly Peace,
holding two million pictures of that face—
as though to answer
the ghosts of all those Mao called
  gentry   landowners
     bourgeois elements,
blood in the river of the Revolution:
How can one say
    that the peasants should not now
rise, and shoot one or two of them
  and bring about
a small-scale reign of terror?

A revolution is not
like inviting people to dinner
  or writing an essay,
    or doing fancy needlework. . . .

I remember the XIVth Dalai Lama
  of what is now
"The Autonomous Cultural Region of Tibet"—
in Delhi in the 60s, in exile.
He steps into a taxi
  in monk's robes, with shaved head.
The swarthy, tribal-looking bodyguards
    break off their card game
        and follow him.

"Place on one side,"
  he says to his visitors,
"the dogs of this neighborhood—
and on the other side, my life.
The lives of the dogs are worth more."

But that day in '76
          I speak of—
everything seemed to rise on one side of life,
          and recede on the other.
I was thirty-five years old.
I ordered a double espresso.
The dust-mottled bust of Dante, now gone,
     glared at me across the bar—
untiring, unresting,
     with his hook nose and predator's eyes.

A newspaper clipping,
San Francisco Chronicle, "The Voice of the West":
"Chinese Radical's Great Leap to Bay Area."

The former Red Guard
stowed away on a boat to Hong Kong . . .
His plaid sofa   his RCA color TV,
his view of San Francisco Bay. . . .
An articulate young man,
he has applied to three law schools,
including Harvard. . . .
Has just sold a $160,000 building.

A certain drive, a certain
          assertiveness . . .
as though the Revolution
          equipped him with the tools
to make it
          in America.

The rainbow trout in my daydream
     flashes in glassy water,
snags the wet fly in mid-riffle,

fights me like a small country.
I play him quiet
        into my quiet hand underwater,
hold him in the current,
        and slip the hook out
                of his hard jaw.

The trout hangs in the current
        as if slow to feel freedom come back
                into his muscles,
then thrashes free downstream.

Aphorisms of Ancient Sun Tzu,
                5th century BC:
Be as swift as the wind, as secret as the forest,
as consuming as fire, as silent as the mountains,
as impenetrable as darkness, as sudden
as thunderbolts.

War is nothing but lies.

In throwing in troops, drop them
like a millstone on an egg,
the solid on the void.

Mr. Giotta turns the café lights on.
It's easy to see
                the dawn now
        as Chu Teh saw it
when the Long March began:
        Over stones and peaks worn
to slippery smoothness
        by no one knows how many
eons of fierce wind, rains, and snow,

58

the column of gaunt and ragged
           men and women,
fleeing Chingkanshan,
   began to creep single-file
along the jagged crest of the
               mountain spur . . .
By nightfall reached a small
sloping ridge of solid volcanic rock
   where we stopped and ate
         half the cold rice we had brought,
   huddling together and linking arms,
passed the night
         shivering and coughing.
With daybreak they crept like fog
   down an overgrown trail
over the first village:
to drop like a millstone on the enemy garrison—
      "the solid on the void."

   Thousands of rifles and machine-guns
lay buried on the long trail south . . .
      much ammunition, much machinery,
               much silver.

From a poem by Mao:
I remember how vivid they were
as they gazed upon rivers and mountains:
The Chinese earth gave strength to their words—
and the ancient feudal lords
were something they scraped off their boots.

I look around the café at faces,
      knowing so many.
Ferlinghetti comes in after work,

59

smiles and frowns at the same time
as if to say:
"Where did we meet?"
A student drinks hot chocolate and reads *Dubliners*.

Ten years ago
we fought all day and ran,
and watched ourselves on network news at night.
The Revolution seemed no farther away
than squadcar blue-lights whipping
hypnotically through fuchsias
in the Berkeley hills—
fear and love in a crowd,
a nose full of teargas,
plate glass heavily smashing.

People say "*Our* Revolution
had its effect."
I yawn, and nod in agreement.
But what I see is
"urban guerillas" cleaning houses,
pumping gas,
cooking eggs at six in the morning
for someone else,
collecting food stamps,
teaching grammar to convicts,
—revolutionized into poverty—
or invisible in some good job.
"The best minds of *my* generation" too,
self-exiled from America,
strangers to power,
a wasted generation.

My teacher from college writes: "Alienation
            hovers over your lines
    like the smell of burning flesh
        over the funeral pyres."

I put a dime in the Trieste's jukebox,
 with its unique selection
of Italian arias   Greek *bouzouki* music
    songs in Portuguese from *Black Orpheus*
        thin-air music from the high Andes
            (bass drum and flute).

Maria Callas sings
        "Un Bel Dì Vedremo."
        Silence sinks into the café.

Remember:
The Chinese earth gave strength to their words.

A last photograph:

5. *Mao Tse-tung swimming the Yangtse River, 1966*
His solemn, chunky head visible
    above water
like the head of an old bull—
showing his enemies himself alive,
Mao floats on his back
    or side-strokes lazily
        crossing the two-mile river
        gazing at the changing sky—
oil refineries on the bank,
        mountains in the far distance:

I've just drunk the waters of Changsha,
now I taste fish in the surf at Wuchang.
Let the wind blow, let rain drench me.
I'd rather be here
than wasting time in rooms of power.
Today I am free!
Old Confucius stands on the bank,
                    observing:
"All nature is flowing away."

New cars slip through Saturday night—
headlights, red tail-lights streaking,
            rain blowing off the ocean.
I walk through North Beach
        beside and beneath neon bodies
            of unreal women.

I light an illegal cigarette
        and smoke it unnoticed through Chinatown,
over hosed-down sidewalks smelling of fish,
past the hot windows of Chinese sweatshops
            open to the night—
live pheasants in cages on the roof of a car,
            heads of cattle in buckets,
leopard sharks in shop-windows on beds of ice.

Mah-jong tiles click in below-street parlors.
    Blue light seeps through closed blinds;
red-and-white uniforms swim over TV grass.

Business picks up again at the Golden Dragon,
where blood of seventeen people
        was washed off the floor last year
and the place remodeled.

I gravitate toward my parking place,
      stepping into the baroque church
      of Our Lady of Guadalupe
to shake two junkies who are following me.

In the fragrant semi-darkness
   I touch cool water to my forehead.
The priest hands me pamphlets
   and asks God to bless me.
He stops me as I leave the church.
"God bless you," he says the second time.
            "Pray for us all."
I promise to do that, and step outside.
      The two men are gone.

I find the car and drive out past
solid, stone-built Pacific Avenue mansions—
past bars for every kind of drinker—
past everybody and everything there is
            to buy—
past a Chinese lady in silk
      looking into the vanished sunset—
past the exquisite
three-hundred-year-old military base—
      white markers, thousands
in a forest of mist and cypresses—
out over the Golden Gate
and the spirits of all the dead.
I nudge my car into the northbound stream, alone,
      straight down the middle of the bridge,
into the redwoods and foothills,
into the open darkness.

San Francisco, 1979